AMAZONIAN LANDSCAPES AND SUNSETS

NORTHWATER

CONSTANTINE ISSIGHOS

Copyright 2012 © Constantine Issighos. Published in Canada. Printed in U.S.A. No part of this book may be reproduced or transmitted in any form or by any means, electronic or mechanical, including photocopying, recording, and/or by any information storage and retrieval system except by a reviewer who may quote brief passages in a review to be printed in a magazine, newspaper, or on the web without written permission in writing from the author/publisher. For information, please contact www.awaqkunabooks.com

NorthWater is an imprint of Awaqkuna Books Inc.

Vol. 9 of THE AMAZON EXPLORATION SERIES:
AMAZONIAN LANDSCAPES AND SUNSETS

Library and Archives Canada

ISBN 978-0-9878599-8-3

Library and Archives Canada Cataloguing in Publication

ATTENTION CHILDRENS ASSOCIATIONS, BOOK STORES, PUBLIC OR PRIVATE LIBRARIES: quantity discounts are available on bulk purchases of this book series.

THE AMAZON EXPLORATION SERIES

Children's Books
by
Constantine Issighos

1	Upper Amazon Voyage by River Boat
2	The People of the River
3	The Children of the River
4	Amazon's Nature of Things
5	Echoes of Nature: a Beautiful Wild Habitat
6	The Amazon Rainforest
7	Amazonian Sisterhood
8	Amazon River Wolves
9	Amazonian Landscapes and Sunsets
10	Amazonian Canopy: the Roof of the World's Rainforest
11	Amazonian Tribes: a World of Difference
12	Birds and Butterflies of the Amazon
13	The Great Wonders of the Amazon
14	The Jaguar People
15	The Fresh Water Giants
16	The Call of the Shaman
17	Indigenous Families: Life in Harmony with Nature
18	Amazon in Peril
19	Giant Tarantulas and Centipedes
20	The Amazon Ethno-Botanical Garden
21	The Real Amazon Tribal Warriors

Imagine yourself canoeing down a narrow winding river surrounded on both sides by a lush, endless landscape of greenery, and all that separates you from the muddy Amazon waters is your dugout canoe built from a single tree trunk. As you drift around a bend something unidentified crashes off into the undergrowth, and you catch a glimpse of two magnificent black caiman startled into hiding. Suddenly, the river surface ahead of you erupts with the gregarious roar of a giant otter devouring its prey, a fierce predator constantly on the prowl.

During your canoe trip, it is easy to spot handsome shore-birds such as herons, kingfishers and ospreys scattered between indigenous huts as you travel steadily away from civilization. However, as you paddle deeper into the rainforest, it is easy to feel that you are the one being watched! As you cross the river, the cries of the birds lead you to your final destination which magically appears out of the jungle at the last possible moment. You look up at the canopy, and you see Common and Brown Capuchin Monkeys, Quetzals and a host of other colourful birds that inhabit the lush greenery of the world's "roof of the rainforest," while a bubbling mountain stream tumbles past the indigenous habitat you've arrived at.

But this morning's biggest water splash belongs to the giants of the aquatic world, the Pink Dolphins. The he largest species of river dolphin, it can grow to a length of up to 2.6 meters (9 feet). As you admire the surrounding landscape along the riverbanks, you may consider this to be a heavenly place. If you were a landscape artist and you wanted to paint the Amazon's vast rainforest, you could be in one of the most beautiful and mysterious locations, one that could artistically inspire you.

When the morning sun clears the tall tree line and strikes the clay riverbanks and undergrowth, one of the world's most amazing wildlife spectacles is nearing its lively peak as hundreds of parrots flock to the clay banks for a grab of clay.

From the forest undergrowth to the canopy, moss covers the tree trunks, and plants upon plants are hanging from every bit of bark. Tiny bird nests can be seen in the creepers and vines which wind their way around the trees. If you pay attention and look closely, you can see the baby birds' miniature mouths opening and closing within these well-hidden nests. Tiny fingers of morning mist trickle through the mossy rocks, ferns and purple-tongued orchids which are suspended in mid-air on flimsy vines. Black or brown winged adult birds with red or yellow bellies fly past to drop off insect food for their chicks every few minutes.

If you are lucky, you may spot in the understory branches of the canopy the magical, mystical, notoriously aloof and wonderfully exotic Amazonian bird, the Quetzal. The beauty of its long green feathers, curving down like a quill from its tiny body, takes your breath away! Of course, looks can be deceptive, for this bird is a chicken-sized relative of the cuckoo bird that cannot fly very well, and smells like cow manure, due to its digestive system.

Perhaps you stop for a moment and ponder this: "Can I be indifferent to the croaks of the frogs and toads at sunset, to the chants of the monkeys in the forest before the evening storms, or to the forcefulness of these storms, the way they impact the forest trees and their role in the lives of the indigenous people? Perhaps you sense that part of your ancestral roots as a human being is here, in the tropics, in a place where you feel an intense sense of smallness, of wonder, and an overwhelming transcendent serenity!

Another beautiful sunset to marvel over the Amazon River! The evening is aflame with beauty. The heavenly colours of the sunset may transport you into a world that transcends your daily existence. The sky takes on a rosy hue. The few clouds overhead are like puffs of pure white snowflakes. I have to admit there is something special about sunsets in the Amazon. I find myself mesmerized watching the sunsets while canoeing on the Maranon river. I find myself contemplating the way things are going on my Amazon journey. It has a calming effect on me. I am a rather solitary person and it's my preference to travel alone the majority of the time in order to reflect, gather my thoughts, and write.

This evening's sunset casts an orange background above the horizon, lighting up the sky as if lit by a flame. In the distance, above the canopy trees, the hanging clouds are splashed with random colours of hot red, with hints of blues and purples. I look at the surrounding web of life, knowing that its beauty and the interdependency of all life in the rainforest is vital to my well-being.

The "fire ball in the sky" seems to whisper farewell to me and my surroundings as it lazily sinks lower and lower, almost as if it did not want to leave me alone! I keep looking at the sun, yet even from beyond the tree line, it seems that is staring at me, a silent flame of wonderment that gives me warmth, life-light and contentment.

I close my eyes for what seems like a moment; my thoughts are fleeting, and when I open my eyes again the sunset is complete, leaving behind a sea of stars and lonely clouds in a twilight sky. As with the Amazon sunsets, I realize that everything has its time to shine, and today is also my time to shine.

The covered motorized canoe travels down the sediment-rich waters of the Maranon River. Dark clouds have been gathering for some time. As I travel, they begin to roll in and darken. When fingers of lightening light up the horizon, I decide to go ashore. The black water of the river is invisible after dark; I try to make out the horizon, but it merges with the sky above.

In this black-water paradise, where you'd least expect to find any sign of people, dugout canoes cross your path, lone fishermen cast their circular nets and the cries of tropical birds serve as your guide to your next destination, the Canopy Walks.

Imagine exploring the canopy scenery from high up in the treetops. It offers an unbelievable opportunity to spot dozens of animals, hundreds of colourful butterflies, including spectacular morphs as they flutter from flower to flower. A canopy walkway is basically a series of suspension bridges connecting emergent trees, with observation platforms on each tree. The canopy walkway serves as part of the growing eco-tourism in the Amazon, as well as a scientific research and educational tool. With unprecedented access to the forest canopy, it provides you with a wonderful opportunity to view the upper level scenery and to study the rich plants and animals of that habitat. Here, I watch the last, frantic activity, or rush hour of the evening, before night settles and the nocturnal life of the Amazon's canopy takes over.

The Amazon landscape is full of memories and stories told by the indigenous people over the centuries. For thousands of years they have told stories about the power of revered landscapes, where the surrounding scenery is full of wildlife, beauty and spiritual directions to mysterious richness and places. Their extended family of the indigenous people includes the rainforest, the sacred places, the cliffs, rivers, hills and mountains. It is a land of myth and magic, a micro cosmos of the timeless and the blessed. The worship of earth, sky and water is still practiced in the Amazon today. Knowledge of the landscape is used to comfort and help the people who seek answers and solutions to the deep questions of their lives. The stories told by the tribal elders are their only form of penetrating beyond the curtain of the visible world, into the sacred place of knowledge and mystery. Through the cultural form of expressing the dialectics of their knowledge, the new indigenous generation can value and interpret these oral stories, both the parts that are strictly personal and the parts that apply to all.

In the morning, before the sun rises in the sky, the jungle's landscape becomes a stage full of sounds and melodies. It seems as if nature's alarm cloak is waking me to witness the moment the colours of the world come alive. The intense glare of the morning's rays is reflected onto the river waters of the world's largest rainforest.

A great sense of being one with the landscape overtakes my senses. As my eyes witness a miraculous moment of Mother Nature, the beginning of a new day! As the bright day passes into night, another Amazonian sunset touches me deeply. The cloud formation permits a radiant glow to pass through, highlighting the intense natural colour of the deep blue sky. I want so much to walk on the clouds!

The Amazon Exploration Series *Constantine Issighos*

Amazonian Landscapes and Sunsets

The Amazon Exploration Series   *Constantine Issighos*

Amazonian Landscapes and Sunsets   *15*

Amazonian Landscapes and Sunsets

The Amazon Exploration Series *Constantine Issighos*

Amazonian Landscapes and Sunsets *19*

The Amazon Exploration Series   *Constantine Issighos*

Amazonian Landscapes and Sunsets   *23*

The Amazon Exploration Series — *Constantine Issighos*

Amazonian Landscapes and Sunsets

The Amazon Exploration Series   *Constantine Issighos*

Amazonian Landscapes and Sunsets

The Amazon Exploration Series   *Constantine Issighos*

Amazonian Landscapes and Sunsets

The Amazon Exploration Series　　　　　　　　　　　　　*Constantine Issighos*

Amazonian Landscapes and Sunsets

The Amazon Exploration Series *Constantine Issighos*

Amazonian Landscapes and Sunsets

The Amazon Exploration Series   *Constantine Issighos*

Amazonian Landscapes and Sunsets

The Amazon Exploration Series   *Constantine Issighos*

Amazonian Landscapes and Sunsets

The Amazon Exploration Series   *Constantine Issighos*

Amazonian Landscapes and Sunsets   *41*

The Amazon Exploration Series *Constantine Issighos*

Amazonian Landscapes and Sunsets

The Amazon Exploration Series   *Constantine Issighos*

Amazonian Landscapes and Sunsets

The Amazon Exploration Series   *Constantine Issighos*

Amazonian Landscapes and Sunsets

The Amazon Exploration Series   *Constantine Issighos*

Amazonian Landscapes and Sunsets

www.ingramcontent.com/pod-product-compliance
Lightning Source LLC
Chambersburg PA
CBHW041754040426
42446CB00001B/31